A Stroll Through

Historic Salem

A Chestnut Street Fencepost

A Stroll Through
Historic Salem

by SAMUEL CHAMBERLAIN

HASTINGS HOUSE   Publishers   NEW YORK

Published simultaneously in Canada by
Saunders, of Toronto, Ltd. Don Mills, Ontario

SBN : 8038-6689-5

Library of Congress Catalog Card Number : 78-79738
Printed in the United States of America

Contents

Washington Square in October.

The author acknowledges with thanks the assistance of several persons and organizations in the preparation of this book, in particular Mrs. Elizabeth Butler Frothingham, Mr. James H. Ballou, The Essex Institute, The Peabody Museum, The House of Seven Gables Settlement Association, and The Salem Maritime National Site.

The following photographs have been reproduced through the courtesy of the Peabody Museum: Pages 7, 8, 35, 65 (both pictures), 66 (all three pictures) and 67 (both pictures). The following photographs have been reproduced through the courtesy of the Essex Institute: Pages 50 (lower), 51 (both pictures), and 58 (top). All other photographs have been taken by the author.

The John Ward House in winter.

Introduction

In this enlightened age, when more and more Americans are exploring their own country, New England is receiving a bounty of visitors. It offers them a refreshing change, with an incomparable coastline, a quiet, radiant countryside and a rich complex of historic towns and villages. People come to New England not only for its beaches, lakes and camping sites. They are attracted primarily by its historical significance. They make pilgrimages to Plymouth, to Lexington and Concord, to Boston and Cambridge, because these names have been imbedded in their minds since their early school days. It is an inspiring experience to travelers who are truly interested in the early history of our country.

For this reason, the venerable seaport of Salem, Massachusetts, intrigues them. The foremost shipping center of the Colonies for decades, and one of the first pioneer settlements in the New

1

World, Salem has welcomed uncounted thousands of appreciative visitors from home and abroad. The city receives them hospitably, opens her museums and old houses to them and provides them with an illustrated folder and map that guides them to the points of interest in the ancient city. Accommodations for travelers are good. Salem is unquestionably one of the highlights of a New England pilgrimage.

Naturally enough, many visitors would like to carry back more than a mental vision of Salem, and this book aspires to give them a richly illustrated record of what they have seen. It also hopes to be their friendly guide and elbow companion as they stroll through its elm-shaded streets and explore its venerable houses.

The early history of Salem goes back to the very dawn of the American colonies. Jamestown, in Virginia, was the forerunner, of course. Plymouth and its courageous *Mayflower* Pilgrims made the year 1620 a milestone in American history. Only three years later, Roger Conant and his gathering of intrepid fishermen crossed the stormy Atlantic and settled on Cape Ann, an exposed outpost on the New England shore.

They found this rocky island rather forlorn. The pasturage for animals was meager, and the harbors for their ships were too open and unprotected. Casting about for a better solution, Conant and his band of adventurers sailed southwest for a few miles and established a new settlement in Naumkeag, where a secluded cove offered a safe haven for their ships and an attractive ridge of land provided a site for their crude temporary dwellings. This was in 1626, and Naumkeag soon became known as Salem.

This was a time of unrest in England, and many worthy citizens, indignant at the acts of the King, chose to leave their homeland and brave the tumultuous Atlantic to find a different life in New England. The Dorchester Company was chartered and in 1628 it organized a colony of settlers under the leadership of Captain John Endecott. (The original charter, incidentally, may be seen in the Essex Institute.) These industrious newcomers lost no time in building substantial shelters on a crude thoroughfare that is now Salem's Washington Street. The "Governor's Fayre House" was built from timbers of an earlier house on Cape Ann. In 1629 "two godly ministers," Francis Higginson and Samuel

The Pickering House (1660), most ancient in Salem.

Skelton, arrived to care for the Puritans and founded the first Congregational Society in America. A church was built in 1635, and the site is marked by a commemorative plaque near the corner of Washington and Essex streets. With the arrival of Governor Winthrop on the Ship *Arbella* in June 1630, bearing the precious charter of the Massachusetts Bay Company, Salem was well on its way to greatness.

Nothing remains of the early dwellings built by the first settlers but a reasonable facsimile can be found in Pioneer Village. This was built three centuries later, in 1930, on a site in Forest River Park, to commemorate the arrival of Governor Winthrop and his brave colonists. This waterside settlement gives a dramatic picture of the habitations, the hardships, the industry and the courage of these brave people.

The latter part of the seventeenth century has bequeathed many authentic architectural treasures, however, and almost all of these are available to visitors. Scattered over Salem are several

3

The Witch House (circa 1662) in a springtime setting.

The Rebecca Nurse House (1678) in Danvers, formerly Salem Village.

venerable Elizabethan structures—the Pickering House on Broad Street, the "Witch House" on Essex Street, the Ward House at the Essex Institute and a group of three ancient buildings gathered at the House of Seven Gables settlement. They provide a graphic and revealing image of the way of life of a new generation of settlers.

The closing years of the seventeenth century brought Salem unwelcome fame. The witchcraft delusion of 1692 is by far the most publicized episode in its history and has been recorded in scores of books. In recent years the dreadful details have been adapted to the theater, to the cinema and to television, giving Salem publicity that its more thoughtful citizens find quite distasteful. However, the appellation "Witch City" still persists, and a witch with a pointed hat and broomstick has come to be a local symbol.

Witchcraft had existed in England and executions for this "crime" had occurred there before the scourge hit Salem. Here it began in the outlying Salem Village, now a part of Danvers, where the minister, Samuel Parris, had brought three slaves from the West Indies. One of them, a superstitious native Indian woman named Tituba, told weird tales to the minister's daughter, aged nine, and many of her older companions. The children reacted by making loud, incoherent noises, going into convulsions and assuming strange positions. These aberrations were probably a form of hysteria rather than deliberate feigning, though some have accused the children of being merely vengeful brats. Dr. Griggs, the village physician, was called to diagnose the case and asserted that the youngsters were bewitched. When pressed to reveal who had bewitched them, they named two innocent persons, Sarah Good, a poverty-stricken woman with several children, and Sarah Osburn, who was feeble-minded and bedridden. Finally they accused Tituba herself. Two Salem magistrates, Jonathan Corwin and John Hathorne, examined the accused at the Meeting House, and committed them to jail. Sarah Good was tried and convicted in Salem and executed on Gallows Hill on July 19, 1692. Another innocent woman who went to her death that day was seventy-year old Rebecca Nurse, a greatly respected mother of a large family. The ghastly period of witchcraft delusion lasted from February

5

The old loom in the Witch House.

1692 to May 1693. During this time nineteen persons were executed, and many others were thrown in jail. One of the victims, octogenarian Giles Corey, was crushed to death under heavy weights.

Citizens of the highest character were accused as the months went by, including even the wife of Governor Phips. This was too much for the governor and he ordered all persons accused of witchcraft released from jail, whether convicted or not. This tardy action on his part eliminated witchcraft as a crime in America, once and for all.

There are a few melancholy reminders of this period in Salem's history. Gallows Hill, where the hangings took place, is virtually unchanged from that day to this. Nathaniel Hawthorne deplored the fact that there was no marker on this desolate spot where so many tragedies occurred. "Yet, ere we left the hill, we could not but regret that there is nothing on its barren summit, no relic of old, no lettered stone of later days, to assist the imaginaion in appealing to the heart. We build a memorial column on the

6

The busy port of Salem, illustrated by the Wharf Diorama in the Peabody Museum.

height which our fathers made sacred with their blood poured out in a holy cause. And here, in dark, funereal stone, should rise another monument, sadly commemorative of the errors of an early race, and not to be cast down, while the human heart has one infirmity that may result in crime."*

An authentic survivor of those days, the home of Judge Corwin, has been restored, furnished with antique pieces and opened to the public under the name of the Witch House. Most moving of all is the home of the martyred Rebecca Nurse, which is still standing on Pine Street in Danvers. A beautiful old timbered house with gables and an overhang, it is open to the public during the warmer months. The library of the Essex Institute has an extensive collection of books on Salem witchcraft for those who wish to delve further into the subject. Other documents are in the Salem courthouse.

In spite of such distressing events, Salem's fame as a seaport was spreading constantly. In addition to the fishermen, sailing

*"Visitor's Guide to Salem" Essex Institute, 1927

7

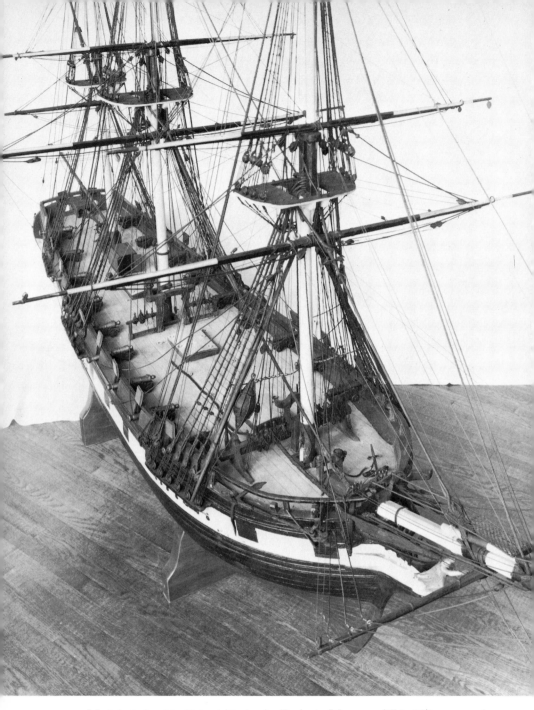

Model of the ship *Friendship* in the Peabody Museum. This 347-ton vessel, built in Salem in 1797, exemplifies the type of ship that was used in Salem's widening ocean trade.

vessels early engaged in direct commerce with England and the West Indies, trading in staves, sarsaparilla, sugar, molasses, logwood and, above all, fish. Dry cod found a ready market in Spain. France and Holland welcomed whalebone, whale and fish oil and furs. The most popular type of sailing vessel putting out from Salem at that time was the ketch, measuring from twenty to forty tons burden and manned by no more than half a dozen youthful sailors. But there were larger ships of eighty to two-hundred tons also. Salem's shipyards hummed with activity.

When the Revolutionary War broke out, the American colonists found themselves faced with a formidable adversary. When Boston and New York were both occupied by the British, the port of Salem assumed sudden importance. Its patriotic citizens perceived the problem and converted their ships into armed privateers. Furthermore they rapidly built new and larger vessels to harrass British shipping. Heavily armed, they took over four-hundred prizes on the sea. With the end of the war, the Salem merchants found themselves owners of large, speedy vessels, too big to serve domestic shipping or even make profitable voyages to Europe. This opened up the possibility of sailing to more distant ports and engaging in barter, a pursuit in which Yankee sailors excelled.

Salem was filled with young, daring seamen, yearning for excitement, and soon the merchant ships of the town were bound for the remote corners of the earth, braving encounters with pirates, cannibals and the armed ships of France and England. With primitive navigational instruments and in some areas practically without charts, these boys, only a few of them out of their teens, managed to sail their vessels to strange shores and to return with valuable cargos. They had to be good salesmen and better buyers, for the success of their voyage depended upon their business acumen. In exchange for fundamental American products such as tobacco, lumber, dried fish, brandy, rum and iron, they brought back such luxuries as silk and tea from China, fabrics from India, coffee from Arabia, pepper and spices from Sumatra.

As the years went by Salem's ships became larger and speedier. Elias Hasket Derby sent his rapid *Grand Turk,* built in 1780-81, to the Cape of Good Hope and soon this vessel was opening up trade with China. Other intrepid sea captains ventured to the East Indies,

Chestnut Street, residential shrine of the sea captains and the merchant shippers of the 19th century.

Russia and Japan. Salem's fame spread far and wide. Derby Wharf, where the ships docked after their long voyages, teemed with activity, exotic odors and strange animals. The first elephant ever seen in the United States was landed here in 1796.

At the dawn of the nineteenth century Salem's commerce was at its peak, but the embargo of 1807 and the War of 1812 had an adverse effect. Nevertheless the merchant seamen pushed on, seeking new outlets in Africa, Australia and South America and building up impressive fortunes during the early decades of the nineteenth century. The opulent mansions that they built in Salem at that time are a testimony to their success. With the discovery of gold in California, Salem shipowners lost no time in sailing prospectors around Cape Horn to San Francisco. But with the advent of new and larger clipper ships, built in mid-century, Salem's supremacy declined dramatically. Her shallow, landlocked harbor was unable to accommodate these new sailing vessels, which were directed to Boston and New York. Derby Wharf lost its animation and its warehouses slumped into decay. The advent of the railroad sounded the death knell to further shipping. Nevertheless, Salem had enjoyed its glorious day as the greatest of all American merchant ports.

Visitors will find abundant reminders of this historic epoch. Although the warehouses have disappeared, Derby Wharf has been restored, as have the notable buildings that stood at its head on Derby Street. These include the original Custom House, the Richard Derby House, the Hawkes House and the Rum Shop. The magnificent Peabody Museum on Essex Street is the most revealing of all. It is filled with curiosities brought back by Salem sea captains from the four corners of the earth, as well as ship models, figureheads, marine paintings and tools of the nautical profession. The great triumphs of Salem shipping come alive with a visit to this museum, hospitably open to the public without charge. Finally there are the luxurious houses built by these successful young sea captains. They are scattered over many parts of Salem but the majority of them are concentrated on Chestnut Street, considered by many authorities to be the noblest thoroughfare in America.

Salem is proud of many distinguished citizens, among them the somewhat austere Governor John Endecott, who arrived from the south of England in 1628. Simon Bradstreet, who landed with

11

This detail of a mantelpiece in the Pingree House shows Samuel McIntire's mastery in carving his famous wheatsheaf.

the Winthrop party on the *Arbella* in June 1630, outlived every-body on the ship, dying at the ripe old age of ninety-four. He was twice governor of the province. His house, a thoroughly Eliza-bethan structure with two overhangs and many gables, was built on the site now occupied by the Essex Institute. Nathaniel Bowditch (1773-1838), the great mathematician and navigational expert, was born in a quaint house on Salem's Brown Street, and in his later years lived in an imposing house on Essex Street near the present "Witch House." He was the author of the *New American Practical Navigator,* a classic volume that has gone through more than sixty editions and is still used under the title of *Bowditch's Navigator.* Alexander Graham Bell, inventor of the telephone, conducted many of his experiments in the Saunders House at 292 Essex Street. The site of the old house, now occupied by the YMCA, is marked by a commemorative plaque. The best known of Salem's sons, however, are Samuel McIntire, the famed wood carver and architect, and Nathaniel Hawthorne, the great novelist, who has earned a pre-eminent place in American letters.

Samuel McIntire, one of the greatest American craftsmen and designers, was born in Salem in 1757. His father, Joseph McIntire, was a capable housewright and taught his three sons, Joseph Jr., Samuel and Angier, the fundamentals of carpentry and wood carving. The three brothers worked as partners for a time, repairing Salem houses, but Samuel stood out from the others for his skill. He soon became the protegé of Elias Hasket Derby, fore-most of Salem merchant-shippers, and undertook a succession of architectural commissions for him. Samuel McIntire avidly studied the existing English books on classical architecture and by his mid-twenties was already a brilliant designer. At that time he drew the plans for a superb three-story mansion for shipowner Jerathmeal Peirce on Federal Street and did a great deal of the wood carving in the paneled rooms. He also carved the decorative urns on the fence posts and made special upholstered benches to fit in the win-dow niches. All of these may still be seen by interested visitors.

His fame spread rapidly, and soon he was designing mansions on Washington Square, a courthouse and a few commercial build-ings. Encouraged by early successes, McIntire entered into a com-petition for planning the Federal Capitol in 1792, and submitted

Fence posts and urns at the Peirce-Nichols House, originally designed and carved by Samuel McIntire.

Doorway of the Clifford Crowninshield House at 74 Washington Square East, designed by Samuel McIntire.

a handsome, if unsuccessful, solution. The influence of Charles Bulfinch and the Brothers Adam was apparent in McIntire's work around 1793. In the opulent Lyman house in Waltham, the only residence McIntire designed outside the vicinity of Salem, there is a superb oval drawing room, very Bulfinch in character. His most ambitious mansion was doomed to a short life. Elias Hasket Derby and his aspiring wife, Elizabeth Crowninshield, embarked upon a magnificent undertaking, incorporating Bulfinch's designs and definitive plans by McIntire, for a Salem residence unparalleled in New England history. In addition to the classic brick mansion with a central stair hall leading to an oval drawing room with an Adam ceiling, there were formal outbuildings and a summer house in the form of a temple. McIntire designed and built a great deal of furniture for the mansion. The Derbys were destined to enjoy their treasure for only a few months. They both died in 1799, and none of their heirs was financially able to keep up the house, which was hopefully offered for sale for years and then finally torn down in 1815. A great deal of the McIntire carving and paneling was salvaged.

14

Samuel McIntire's exquisite summerhouse, designed for the Derbys and now installed at Glen Magna Farms in Danvers.

Thus one of McIntire's great accomplishments has virtually dissappeared, but many others remain. He designed a delightful little two-storied summer house for the Derbys, adorned with sculptured figures. It can now be seen in the grounds of Glen Magna Farms in Danvers. Everything else he designed was for his native Salem. In 1804 he produced plans for the beautiful South Church on Chestnut Street. This graceful edifice, whose spire revealed the strong influence of Sir Christopher Wren, was gutted by fire in 1903, almost a century later. At the peak of his career, McIntire designed several notable brick buildings, among them Hamilton Hall, which has been for more than a century and a half the citadel of social life in Essex County. The beautiful brick Pingree House, built in 1804, may be considered his culminating masterpiece.

15

Nathaniel Hawthorne's birthplace in its new setting overlooking Salem Harbor.

Samuel McIntire died in 1811 at the early age of fifty-four, after which his work was carried on by his son, Samuel Field McIntire. There are abundant evidences of the genius of Salem's architect-carver scattered over the city and his finest buildings are open to the public. Despite the fact that he rarely left his native city, very little of McIntire's personal life is available to historians. Aside from bills for his services (all remarkably reasonable) no letters signed by him have been found. But his handiwork is everywhere in Salem.

No such mystery surrounds the life of Nathaniel Hawthorne, whose writings were prolific and whose activities have been closely followed by historians. The great American novelist was born in Salem on July 4, 1804, in an attractive gambrel-roofed house at 27 Union Street. In recent years this house has been moved to a site overlooking Salem Harbor and now forms a part of the House of Seven Gables group.

16

The "Old Manse" in Concord (1769), early residence of the young Hawthornes.

Young Nathaniel left Salem at the age of four, when his widowed mother moved to South Casco, a small town near Sebago Lake in Maine. Most of his early years were spent in that state. He graduated from Bowdoin College in the Class of 1825, two of his classmates being Henry Wadsworth Longfellow and Franklin Pierce, who was destined to become President of the United States. The young graduate decided upon a literary career and returned to his native Salem, where he led a lonely and secluded life in a rather shabby house on Herbert Street. He wrote industriously for some twelve years, polishing his prose and perfecting his gifts as an imaginative romanticist. *Twice Told Tales* was one of his earliest works and it marked him for future fame. To fortify an author's slender budget, he worked in 1839 as a measurer in the Boston Custom House. It was a dull occupation but Hawthorne took consolation in the fact that both Chaucer and Robert Burns had once been custom-house officers.

In 1842 Hawthorne married his childhood playmate, Sophia Amelia Peabody, whose family lived in the Grimshawe House, adjoining the Old Burying Point on Charter Street. It was a happy marriage but strangely Hawthorne made most unpleasant allusions to the house in *Dr. Grimshawe's Secret.* The young couple soon moved to Concord, where they lived in the weather-beaten "Old Manse," built in 1769 by the Reverend William Emerson, the "fighting parson" of Concord. His eminent grandson, Ralph Waldo Emerson, visited the old house and the two men of letters became friends. Soon Hawthorne had published *Mosses from an Old Manse,* a collection of memorable short stories.

Still obliged to seek added income, Hawthorne returned to Salem, where he was appointed surveyor of the port. He occupied an office on the lower floor of the Custom House and worked at a stiff, uncompromising wooden desk, which is now in its original setting. Hawthorne drew heavily upon this experience as the background for the early pages of *The Scarlet Letter,* considered to be his greatest work. So vivid were his descriptions of the characters in the Custom House that visitors today ask to see Surveyor Pue's historic document and the embroidered letter "A" itself. Hawthorne wrote this novel while living with his family in a three-story house at 14 Mall Street, a short thoroughfare that leads northward from Salem Common. The house is still standing, but it is not beautified by a facing of staggered asbestos shingles.

Far more celebrated in the minds of visitors is the House of Seven Gables on Turner Street, a romantic structure just over 300 years old that is identified with Hawthorne's great romance of the same name. Miss Susan Ingersoll, Hawthorne's cousin, lived in the ancient house and he was a frequent visitor.

Hawthorne and his family moved again to Concord in 1852, where he bought a house belonging to the famous Alcott family and renamed it "The Wayside." European travels soon ensued as he was appointed Consul at Liverpool during the presidency of his friend Franklin Pierce. Then he traveled widely in France and Italy, where he wrote *The Marble Faun.* Returning to America and Concord, he built an attic hideout in "The Wayside" and here he wrote *Tanglewood Tales.*

Throughout his life Hawthorne was a shy and retiring man. In his Salem youth he stayed close to his room by day and roamed the streets, unrecognized, at night. When fame brought admirers to his door he fled whenever possible. His home life was a happy one, with none of the morbid overtones that haunted some of his novels. Worried about his deteriorating health and not wishing to alarm his family, Nathaniel Hawthorne embarked on a trip to the White Mountains in 1864 and put up for the night in the Pemigewasset House in Plymouth, New Hampshire. There he died peacefully. His native city of Salem has not forgotten him. A fine bronze figure of the great novelist, the work of Bela Pratt, stands in the central green of Hawthorne Boulevard. The Essex Institute is rich in memorabilia of his early years. The places where he lived and worked may be seen by the thousands of visitors who have read his books. Salem's supreme literary figure is the source of its greatest pride.

The Hawthorne Monument by Bela Pratt.

Summer Street.

The passage of the centuries has not been altogether kind to Salem. The industrial age has swept away many of its fine old houses and created empty gaps that are now inevitably black-topped and converted into parking spaces. The disastrous Salem fire of June 1914 laid waste a vast area of more than two-hundred-and-fifty acres. Fortunately few historic structures lay in the path of the flames.

Today Salem is admittedly dull in some spots and inspiring in others, in company with so many historic American cities. In the selective tour that follows, we propose to skip the nondescript and concentrate on the historic treasures of the city. An inquisitive student may forage about and find endless details that we have not mentioned. But the essentials are here. We propose to take you first of all (in your own car) to Pioneer Village, a reconstituted glimpse of a New England settlement of the early 1600s. Following this, the architectural treasures of Salem are visited, along with its museums and churches. Finally we urge you to take a stroll with us through Salem's stately residential streets—Federal, Essex, Chestnut and Broad, stopping to admire the dwellings of the young sea captains and merchant princes who flourished in the nineteenth-century Salem. Whether you take this relaxing tour by "shank's mare" or by Detroit's more effortless locomotion, the result is sure to be happy.

20

Pioneer Village, a re-creation of primitive New England.

Pioneer Village

Salem's early history and privations can now be visualized, thanks to Pioneer Village, an accurate reconstruction of a primitive community in the New England wilderness. It was constructed in 1930 to commemorate the 300th anniversary of Governor Winthrop's arrival in Salem on the Ship *Arbella*.

Pioneer Village is one landmark that is not within "easy strolling distance" in Salem. Located at Forest River Park, near the southern extremity of the city, it can best be reached by motoring southward on Lafayette Street and turning left on Clifton Street, where a Pioneer Village marker is placed. Facing a pond is a group of crude dwellings, dominated by the two-storied "Governor's Fayre House," an interpretation of the 1630 home of Governor John Endecott. It is roofed with massive hand-hewn shingles and its external walls are faced with pine boards showing the markings of a vertical pit saw worked by two stalwart colonists. The windows are set with small diamond panes and the central brick chimney contains two massive fireplaces, the unique protection from the rigors of a New England winter. The smaller cottages are mostly one-room buildings with steep thatched roofs and one huge stone fireplace with a chimney sometimes

21

The "Governor's Fayre House" at Pioneer Village.

The salt works at Pioneer Village, used for evaporating sea water with the aid of a wood fire.

encased in wood—far from a fireproof arrangement. There are also crude wigwams faced with wide slabs of bark and log dugouts built into the hillside. Primitive facilities for salt making, soap rendering, fish drying and boat building are also here. There are brick kilns, and there is a pit for lumber sawing. The herbs and flowers that flourished in the seventeenth century still grow in the gardens.

Isolated by a girdle of trees, this settlement creates an extraordinary image of the pioneer's daily life. Pioneer Village is open to visitors during the summer months and guides in costume are on hand to make your visit more agreeable. There is a slight admission fee. Parking facilities are good. A somewhat fanciful reproduction of the ship *Arbella* once lay here at the harbor's edge but it has disappeared.

The primitive buildings of Pioneer Village face a tranquil, reed-bordered duck pond.

In front of Arbella House is a soap cauldron, suspended from a crude tripod, where grease and lye were boiled.

"The Gables" after a February storm.

The House of Seven Gables

This Elizabethan structure was built near the water's edge in 1668 by Captain John Turner. Three generations of Turners lived here until it was sold to the Ingersoll family in 1782. The Ingersolls, relatives of the Hawthornes, occupied the house for three generations also. Miss Susan Ingersoll, Nathaniel Hawthorne's cousin, lived in the house with her adopted son in the 1840s. The noted author was one of the few men allowed to cross the threshold and his cousin Susan is supposed to have taken him to the attic and shown him the beams and mortices to prove that the house once had seven gables. The novelist apparently liked "The House of Seven Gables" as a title for his romance, which was then in its final stages, and adopted it for his work. Generations of American school children have since read

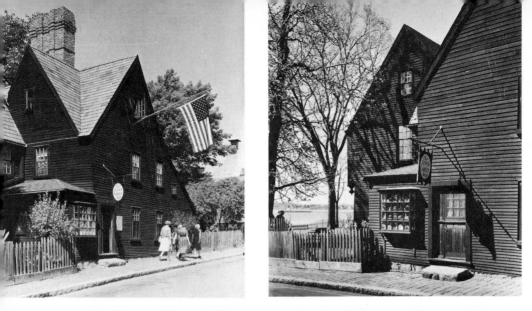

The House of Seven Gables on a summer day. Only two gables are visible here. The simple entrance, whose threshold is crossed by thousands annually, once served as a toll house for the Marblehead ferry.

the book and it is not surprising that this old house is the most celebrated and most visited among all those in historic Salem.

It was restored to its original condition in 1909, through the generosity of Miss Caroline O. Emmerton, and now receives thousands of visitors annually. Their admission fees help support a non-profit philanthropic organization dedicated to settlement work in a predominantly Polish neighborhood.

To reach the House of Seven Gables, drive or walk eastward along Derby Street to Turner Street. Turn right and at No. 54, at the end of Turner Street, you will find the old house. The rooms of this ancient dwelling are furnished with period pieces and some of them retain their superb paneling, mantelpieces, silver and china. It is a memorable experience to explore the old house and its secret staircase leading to "Clifford's room" and the attic. Visitors enter through a ground-floor shop that once served as a tollhouse for the Salem-Marblehead ferry. There is an admission charge and parking facilities have recently been greatly enlarged.

The House of Seven Gables is one of a group of old houses that have been assembled on the shore of Salem Harbor facing Naugus Head. They are clustered around an oldfashioned flower garden, with each having something different to offer the visitor.

The parlor of the House of Seven Gables is marked by discreet pilasters and arched cupboard doors. Over the fireplace hangs a portrait of Mrs. Daniel Sargent, daughter of John Turner III.

In the dining room is a Hepplewhite sideboard and a William and Mary armchair where Dr. Pyncheon, in Hawthorne's novel, was found dead by the butcher boy.

The fireplace of the old kitchen has a built-in brick oven with an early wooden door. On the hearth are two "kitchens" for roasting meat and a few foot-warmers.

The upstairs chamber, known as "Phoebe's Room" in Hawthorne's novel, has a fine early walnut chest of drawers and a Queen Anne highboy.

A winter view of the Retire Becket House, framed in frosted branches. Its roofline is obviously not the original. Shoppers have their moment of relaxation in a store in this ancient house.

Most ancient is the Retire Becket House, which dates back to 1655. For six generations it was the home of the Beckets, a famous family of ship designers and builders. It was rescued from the wreckers in 1924 and today it serves as a gift shop and a place to buy books, postcards, slides and souvenirs. Adjoining it is the Hathaway House, built in 1682 and known for centuries as "the Old Bakery." Hathaway bread was famous in New England but its birthplace was consigned to the wreckers in 1911 in a frightful condition. Miss Emmerton and her friends stepped in at the crucial moment, rescued the ancient house and moved it to a charming site overlooking the harbor. The old paneled kitchen is a room of great beauty, embellished with fine pine woodwork, a noble brick fireplace and a good display of ancient pewter.

The most recent addition to this venerable group is Nathaniel Hawthorne's birthplace, which formerly stood at 27 Union Street. A gambrel-roofed house of pleasing lines, it has been moved to a site near the water's edge within the past few years. Thoroughly restored and furnished with old New England pieces, it is now rich in memorabilia of Salem's great author and serves as a fitting climax to a visit to this weather-stained cluster of old houses.

There are facilities for tired travelers near the garden and during the summer months a charming little restaurant with an open-air terrace serves simple but delectable luncheons.

29

A springtime view of the Hathaway House (1682) facing Salem harbor.

The kitchen of the Hathaway House displays a fine collection of pewter and kitchen utensils.

The birthplace of Nathaniel Hawthorne is a double gambrel-roofed house that once stood on Union Street. It is faced with red painted clapboards.

The simple kitchen fireplace is one of several in Hawthorne's birthplace.

Crowninshield's Wharf, Salem. This is the right-hand half of a painting by George Ropes, now in the Peabody Museum.

The Salem Maritime National Historic Site

A debt of gratitude is owed to the Federal Government for establishing this site in 1938, thus preserving for posterity a group of historic buildings and two wharves associated with Salem's extraordinary maritime activity in the eighteenth century. Administered by the National Park Service, U. S. Department of the Interior, the site is situated on Derby Street where the famous Derby Wharf extends nearly two thousand feet into the harbor. Once built up with storage warehouses and the scene of intense activity, this wharf could accommodate scores of vessels at one time. Neglected for decades and fallen into disrepair, Derby Wharf has now been restored and opened to visitors. It follows an irregular, faintly hooklike pattern into the harbor and the end is marked by a squat, square lighthouse.

Richard Derby began building the wharf about 1766 and during the Revolution his son, Elias Hasket Derby, used it to fit

The Custom House (1819).

The Benjamin W. Crowninshield House, designed by Samuel McIntire in 1810, adjoins the Custom House. President Monroe was once a guest here.

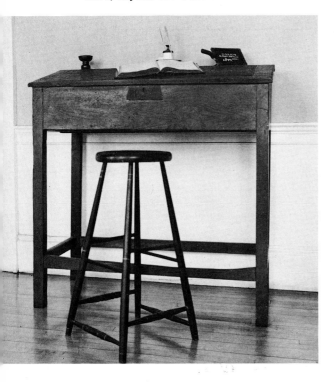

Hawthorne's desk, which he used when serving as Surveyor of the Port of Salem.

out privateers to harass British shipping. From this point in 1784 sailed Derby's vessel *Light Horse,* the first American vessel to visit Russia and the Baltic Sea. The *Grand Turk,* also built by Mr. Derby, set out about the same time to round the Cape of Good Hope and to barter American products for rare and exotic commodities from the Orient.

Numerous warehouses, used to store newly imported cargoes, once stood on the land end of the wharf but they have disappeared. Many sailing vessels, including the second *Grand Turk* and the brig *Henry* were built in shipyards based on Derby Wharf. At its heyday it was the scene of the greatest activity.

Adjoining it was Central Wharf, also touching on Derby Street but only about a third as long. Facing the harbor on the North Side of Derby Street are four buildings from that great era—the Custom House, the frame Hawkes House, the Derby House and a small building called the Rum Shop. The whole area covers about nine acres, and is handsomely landscaped. There are rest facilities for weary travelers in the garden, and adequate parking is provided.

Surmounted by a magnificent gilded eagle, the Custom House stands impressively at the head of Derby Wharf. A gracious brick structure with a fine flight of granite steps and an imposing porch supported by graceful Corinthian columns, it was built in 1819 as headquarters for the customs revenue officers. Its semi-circular entrance doorway is framed in glass and on the floor above is a Palladian window. Built on the site of the homestead of George Crowninshield, whose son was once secretary of the Navy, the Custom House was built for the princely sum of $36,000. It was a wise investment, for in the prosperous years that followed, the Salem Custom House took in an imposing proportion of the national income.

Nathaniel Hawthorne served here as surveyor of the Port of Salem from 1846 to 1849, and the desk at which he wrote still remains in place in the southwestern front room where he worked. Hawthorne gathered material for *The Scarlet Letter* during his leisure moments as a customs officer and he painted a vivid word picture of the Custom House and its occupants in the introduction to his greatest novel.

Springtime view of the Hawkes House, showing a fine McIntire doorway.

The three-story frame Hawkes House was begun by McIntire and finished in 1801.

Across the hallway from Hawthorne's office is an exhibit of ship models and maps that graphically recall Salem's glorious shipping days, when its vessels wandered as far east as Canton, Isle of France, Bombay and Java Head, as well as the Mediterranean ports. Recently opened in the garden behind the Custom House is an authentic scale house for weighing imports. The Custom House and its exhibits are open to the public without charge.

The Derby House, built by one of Salem's most famous sea captains and merchants, Richard Derby, is the oldest brick house in Salem. He built the house in 1761-62 for his equally celebrated son, Elias Hasket Derby, whose exploits during the Revolution included fitting out armed privateers to prey upon British shipping. The house was built in the early eighteenth-century style that the Derbys preferred. Later the old mansion was occupied by another famed sailor, Captain Henry Prince, who made the first voyage to the Philippines by an American vessel.

Sitting serenely at the head of Derby Wharf, the house was suffering from neglect and indifference until it was rescued in 1927 by the Society for the Preservation of New England Antiquities.

Street façade of the Derby House in autumn. Very Georgian in feeling, it is the oldest brick house in Salem. (Below) Rear view of the Derby House, framed in spring foliage.

The Southwest bedroom of the Derby House is notable for its fine paneling.

The dining room of the Derby House has a fine corner cupboard and gate-leg table.

They generously donated the house to the Historic Site ten years later. The fine old paneled rooms have been restored. The original painted colors have been determined and are used in the interiors, which are very beautiful. Some of the furniture and family portraits recall the days when the great Elias Hasket Derby lived here. A visit to these finely appointed rooms is an adventure long to be remembered. There is a modest admission fee for a guided tour of the house.

Adjoining the Derby House on the west is the Hawkes House, a dignified three-story frame mansion designed about 1780 by Salem's great architect-builder, Samuel McIntire. The house was also built for Elias Hasket Derby but it was never completed by him and lay in an unfinished condition for many years. Finally in 1801 the house was bought by Captain Benjamin Hawkes, well known as a merchant and shipbuilder, and he completed the building in its current form. At the present time it is not open to visitors.

The Rum Shop was moved from its original setting at the head of Derby Wharf, where it served as a tavern for many years. Erected about 1800, it filled a needed place in a seafaring

The Southeast parlor of the Derby House is a handsomely paneled room, its woodwork painted a rich olive green. The desk-on-frame at the right dates from about 1700.

The Southeast blue bedroom of the Derby House contains a rare small portable desk and a fine mahogany broken-arch high chest.

The Rum Shop served for many years as a tavern for lonely sailors.
The ancient Narbonne House on Essex Street will soon be restored.

community and brought solace to sailors long at sea. Rumor has it that other consolations awaited the lonely sailor on the second floor. These have long since disappeared, as the whole building now serves as an antique shop.

A recent acquisition of the Historic Site is the ancient Narbonne House at 71 Essex Street. Its rear garden adjoins that of the Historic Site property, and some day the house will be restored and added to it. Built before 1671, it is an interesting saltbox type. The small door at the left led to a "cent shop" squeezed under the lean-to roof.

The Benjamin W. Crowninshield House, an imposing brick edifice designed in 1810 by Samuel McIntire at the twilight of his career, stands just west of the Custom House at 180 Derby Street. Crowninshield was a member of Congress and Secretary of the Navy under Madison and Monroe. The latter president was once a house guest here during his visit to Salem in 1817. Today the old mansion serves as a home for aged women.

Lighthouse, Derby Wharf.

The Forrester House is one of several stately brick mansions that face the north side of Washington Square.

The playing fields in autumn, Washington Square.

Washington Square

The Salem Common, "appointed as a place in which persons may shoot at a mark forever," was set aside in 1685. The area contained about eight acres. There were five ponds and several hillocks here, a fine place for grazing cows and goats. The cowherd, a bonded town functionary, brought animals here daily and returned them to their owners at night. Later the ponds were filled and the land was leveled to become a training field. It was also a place for public demonstration. An old document relates that in September 1768 a man named Row informed the British that a vessel in Salem harbor was about to elude the payment of duty. A crowd gathered and seized citizen Row, took him to the Salem Common, tarred and feathered him and wrote "Informer" on his back. Then they told him to leave town. Needless to say, the Common served as a training field for the local citizens during the Revolution.

43

The opulent Andrew-Safford House dominates the western side of Washington Square.

Graceful frame dwellings, many with central chimneys, border the eastern side of Washington Square.

The Common was renamed Washington Square in 1802. Three years later a wooden fence was provided, with impressive gates. One of the gates was embellished with a wood medallion portrait of George Washington, carved by none other than Samuel McIntire. The medallion is now in the Essex Institute.

Today this is a recreation spot for the young and old of Salem and it has long served as a field for sports. Near the center is an octagonal bandstand, built in 1926. Facing Washington Square on the north are several distinguished brick mansions, one of which serves as a local club and another as a home for aged men. At one corner is the Andrew-Safford House, once considered the most costly mansion in New England. It now belongs to the Essex Institute. A few of Samuel McIntire's stately wooden mansions face the eastern side of Washington Square. With central chimneys and exquisite doorways they bear the unmistakable imprint of the master.

George Washington medallion carved by Samuel McIntire.

Reposing demurely behind trees, the Essex Institute lies along Essex Street between the Armory and the Pingree House.

The Essex Institute

Essex County in Massachusetts, historically one of the most fascinating counties in the nation, is the inspiration for a truly extraordinary organization, the Essex Institute. An art gallery, museum, library, publishing house and lecture forum all in one, it offers a rich experience to visitors who cross its hospitable door-step. If they are interested in early American furniture, portraits by such American masters as Copley, Stuart, Trumbull or Black-burn, antique silver, china and glass objects from our early history, they will be abundantly rewarded here. The extent of the exhibits is far too varied to be listed in detail. The library is especially rich in genealogy and local history and has one of the world's finest collections of books in English on China. Scholars and researchers find a warm welcome in its reading rooms.

There are period rooms and collections of early costumes and uniforms. Treasures are found in the manuscript section, among them the Sheffield patent dated 1623 and one of the two original copies of the Massachusetts Bay Charter of 1628-29. The Essex Institute is free to the public and is open daily throughout the year except on Mondays and certain holidays.

Another of the Institute's admirable functions is to rescue, restore and furnish old Salem dwellings and to open them to the public. Here on the Institute grounds are the Pingree House (1804), considered to be Samuel McIntire's finest brick house, the Crowninshield-Bentley House and the ancient Ward House, dating from 1684. On Federal Street are two other notable mansions, the Peirce-Nichols House (1782), McIntire's early masterpiece, and the Assembly House, a celebrated Salem club where both Lafayette and Washington were entertained.

At the rear of the Essex Institute is an attractive garden planted with old-time flowers. The small Lye-Tapley shoemaker's shop is located here, complete with cobbler's equipment from about 1830. Next to it is a building said to be the first Quaker meeting house in Salem, built in 1688, a quite small building that is now called the Vaughn Doll House. It contains a notable collection of dolls, toys and miniature furniture and is a joy to children.

Against the garden walls of the main building have been installed three ancient and notable doorways. One of them is from the "Dr. Grimshawe House" that adjoins the Old Burying Point on Charter Street, and was vividly described by Nathaniel Hawthorne. His childhood playmate, Sophia Amelia Peabody, who later became his wife, lived in the Grimshawe House. Another doorway, graceful and elliptical, came from the Tucker-Rice House, built about 1809. Still standing almost opposite the Essex Institute on Essex Street, this brick building was designed by Samuel McIntire. A third doorway, recently installed against a new wing, is later in period, with elaborate Ionic columns. It comes from the Joseph Peabody House, which stood on the site of the adjacent Armory.

The Andrew-Safford House at 13 Washington Square adjoins the other Essex Institute properties. It was built in 1818 by John

Doorway from the Tucker-Rice House (ca. 1809), designed by Samuel McIntire.

Doorway from the Joseph Peabody House, once on Essex Street.

Andrew at great cost. At present it is used as the residence of the Director of the Essex Institute. A most unusual balustrade treatment crowns the cornice. The house has a pleasant garden and one corner of the building is a recessed porch supported by four extremely tall Doric columns.

The Crowninshield-Bentley House stood on a site on Essex Street adjoining the present Hawthorne Hotel and was moved to its present location on the Essex Institute property in recent years. The house was built by John Crowninshield in 1727. The Reverend William Bentley, celebrated clergyman and diarist, boarded here with the Crowninshields from 1791 until his death in 1819. The finely paneled rooms of the old house, now furnished with antiques of the period, will be admired by all enthusiasts of old furniture.

Considered the finest brick residence designed by Samuel McIntire, the Pingree House was built for Captain John Gardner in 1804. It reveals the ultimate skill that McIntire lavished on his mantels, cornices, dados, doorways and stair rails, and may be considered his finest achievement. The three-story mansion, acquired in the 1830s by David Pingree, stayed for decades in the Pingree family until it was bequeathed to the Essex Institute, where McIntire's original plan is still preserved.

The Andrew-Safford House in winter, a garden view.

The Crowninshield-Bentley House in its new location.

The paneled west parlor is handsomely furnished.

Two views of the room occupied by Dr. William Bentley, Salem's celebrated clergyman and diarist, who boarded for decades in the Crowninshield-Bentley House.

Under the new ownership the house has been carefully restored, furnished with flawless taste and opened to the public. During the Victorian period many of McIntire's wooden mantles were replaced by marble ones but the originals were found safely stored in the attic, together with the decorative stair rails. A glimpse of the opulence and good taste of Salem's wealthy ship-owners and merchants is afforded by this superb pink brick mansion on Essex Street. It is open to visitors throughout the year; a modest admission fee is charged.

The John Ward House, a fine seventeenth-century dwelling with an Elizabethan overhang, once stood on St. Peter Street in Salem and was moved to the grounds of the Essex Institute in 1910. Carefully restored and furnished, it is now open to visitors during the spring and summer months. There is a small admission fee.

Dating from 1684, this was originally a small house built around a single chimney. Later it was doubled in size, and then a lean-to was added. The interior is quite varied, containing a weaving room, an apothecary's shop and a "cent shop" well stocked with early mechandise, including toys and candy for the children. The kitchen is rich in seventeenth-century atmosphere. The table is set with wooden plates and a fine collection of pewter is assembled on the pine dresser. The dining room is more formal, with a gateleg table and William and Mary chairs.

In the garden is the cupola from the Pickman-Derby-Brookhouse mansion, built about 1790. It is exceptional, because it contains a fresco by Michel Félice Corné, the Italian marine painter who came to Salem in the eighteenth century and left many fine examples of his work.

The Pingree House (1804), McIntire's finest brick residence.

The entrance hall provides a glimpse of McIntire's stair rail, cornice and carved doorway.

The graceful semi-elliptical doorway of the Pingree House is one of McIntire's best.

The front parlor contains a superb mantlepiece and a Hepplewhite card table.

An identical mantlepiece in the rear parlor is embellished by three fine Lowestoft vases. The French wallpaper was designed by Fragonard *fils* in 1808. In the dining room (below) Sheraton chairs surround the table, which holds a candelabra on a French mirrored plateau.

The northeast bedroom of the Pingree House is a study in poise and balance. Delft jars brighten the mantlepiece. The Crowninshield Memorial bedroom (below) has great dignity, enlivened by a pleasant wall group built around an old banjo clock.

The Shaw Memorial room in the Pingree House is finished in robin's-egg blue. A Martha Washington armchair sits by the graceful mantle. The boy's bedroom on the third floor (below) is embellished by old French scenic paper.

Of particular interest to children is the Vaughn Doll House, containing an authentic collection of dolls, toys and miniature furniture from other centuries.

The Vaughn Doll House is an ancient building, said to be the first Quaker Meeting House in Salem, dating from 1688.

The interior of the Lye-Tapley shoemaker's shop. This modest frame building (below) stands unostentatiously in the Essex Institute garden.

Nearby is the John Ward House (1684), a fine early gabled dwelling, seen here in early spring. It contains many curious rooms (below) including a "cent" shop offering everything from candy to drygoods, and an apothecary's shop dating from about 1830.

The kitchen of the John Ward House re-creates the atmosphere of the 17th century down to the smallest detail. The table and pine dresser hold pewter and wooden plates. The kitchen fireplace (below) is spanned by a heavy oak lintel and has a jack for turning the roasting spit.

St. Peter's Church (Episcopal), built in 1833. In the tower hangs the oldest bell in Salem, first rung in 1740, and cast in Gloucester, England.

Peabody Museum

There is no better way of realizing Salem's greatness as a seaport and a center of far-flung shipping and commerce with the Orient than to visit the Peabody Museum, an admirable institution dedicated to Salem's early maritime prowess. It is an outgrowth of a collection of curiosities gathered by a group of Salem sea captains and merchants from the four corners of the earth. They founded the East India Marine Society in 1799 and the present imposing stone East India Marine Hall was built in 1824. Many additions have been built to accommodate the increasing collections, which are now truly remarkable.

In 1867 the Museum was named for George Peabody, noted as a philanthropist, who was born in Salem and died in London. Those who love the sea and those inland visitors who have never had a chance to know it well will be equally enthralled by the scope and variety of the Peabody Museum. In the very first room they will find superlative large-scale models of sailing vessels and a graphic diorama (a recent acquisition) that portrays the wharfside activities when a ship from the Orient was unloaded next to the commodious warehouses such as once flourished on Derby Wharf. The exciting life of the whaler is illustrated by models, paintings and scrimshaw and there are portraits of famous Salem skippers and their ships, many painted in the Orient, some in oil, some in watercolor. All the instruments and tools of the nautical profession are shown. There are simulated underwater exhibits of fish, mammals and reptiles and a most beautiful collection of Essex County birds. On the second floor are figureheads from sailing vessels and an extraordinary display of Chinese export porcelain. Salem's sea captains collected treasures from Polynesia and Micronesia, and these make up memorable exhibits, together with one of the world's finest collections of Japanese ethnological objects. Finally, and unforgettably, is the reproduction of the saloon of Captain George Crowninshield, Jr.'s famous yacht, *Cleopatra's Barge,* with a glimpse of the owner's stateroom and paintings of his ship.

To sum it up, the Peabody Museum is a major attraction for all visitors, young and old, who can spend happy and rewarding hours here. It is open daily, and is free to all.

The East India Marine Hall (1824) now serves as the Peabody Museum.

A vivid picture of the great shipping days at Derby Wharf has been created by this diorama in the Peabody Museum. On the second floor is the Marine Hall (below) with fine ship models, marine paintings and figureheads.

Captain George Crowninshield's stateroom on his famous yacht, *Cleopatra's Barge*. Below is a charming figure by Skillins in the Crowninshield Room, and a liquor chest worthy only of the skipper himself.

Of the scores of ship models in the Peabody Museum, this model of the U.S.S. *Constitution* holds patriotic appeal. Below is a painting of the U.S. Frigate *Essex*.

The Old Burying Point

The Charter Street Burial Ground, most ancient in the city and one of the oldest in the country, dates from 1637. At that time a windmill also occupied this elevated plot of land. This tranquil enclosure will yield treasures to those who like to browse among old gravestones. Hawthorne mentioned it often in his writings. Here is the tomb of Captain Richard More, who crossed on the *Mayflower* as a boy, the only known gravestone of a Mayflower passenger. Adjoining it is the stone of his second wife, Jane.

Timothy Lindall, a prominent Salem merchant, has a beautifully carved headstone with a skeleton and a plump figure of Father Time with his scythe. Governor Simon Bradstreet occupies a large tomb at the highest point of the cemetery. Chief Justice Lynde, Judge Hathorne, of the witchcraft court, and Samuel McIntire, Salem's great architect-craftsman, are all buried here. Some of the most beautiful carved stones commemorate citizens long since forgotten.

The graphic headstone of Timothy Lindall, Salem merchant. Below at the left is the simple headstone of Captain Richard More, Mayflower pilgrim, and the finely chiseled stone of Elizabeth Mansfield.

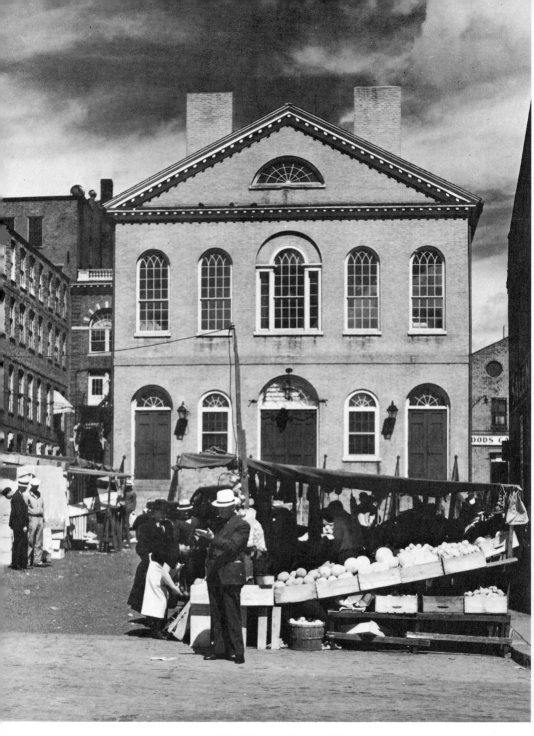

The Market House (1816).

The Market at Town House Square

The Market House was erected on the site of the Elias Hasket Derby House, which was designed by Samuel McIntire, and conceded to be the most magnificent mansion ever built in Salem. It was only occupied for a short time and after Mr. Derby's death it waited, empty and forlorn, for a new buyer. No one wealthy enough to keep it in its original splendor ever appeared and after a few years the great house was torn down. Many of its architectural details, paneling, doorways and mantels, found their way into other Salem houses.

The graceful brick Market House was erected in its place in 1816. It was used for public gatherings and other town purposes, and now on market day it presents a scene of great activity, probably the most picturesque spot in Salem.

The Stephen Daniels House on Essex Street was built in 1667 by a Salem seafaring man. Later enlarged, it still retains two of the original massive stone fireplaces.

Built in 1837, the City Hall is a solid granite building of Greek Revival style.

The Tabernacle Church (Congregational) is a fine Colonial stone structure dedicated in 1924.

The City Hall

The solid structure at 93 Washington Street dates back to the happy time when the government was running a surplus rather than a deficit. Erected in 1837, this dignified granite building was achieved without taxing the city. Instead it was built from the surplus revenue of the United States Treasury, which was distributed to the towns and cities. Above the flat pediment stands a magnificent gilded eagle, a copy of the original carved by Samuel McIntire that had suffered from years of exposure.

Those who are interested in historic documents may see here the original deed for all the land of the town, which the heirs of Chief Nanepashemet turned over for the modest consideration of twenty pounds. The original records of Salem from 1634 to the present time may be seen in the City Clerk's office. There are portraits of Leverett Saltonstall, the first mayor of the city, Lafayette, Washington and Andrew Jackson, among many others.

Federal Street and the façade of the Cook-Oliver House.

A Stroll on Federal Street

The business community that lies between the City Hall and North Street to the west has all but obliterated any sign of old Salem. Here and there is the shell of a fine old brick building, defaced by a modern shop front. Along Federal Street, however, are the Court House and the Registry of Deeds, not remarkable for their architecture but for the documents they contain. In the brick courthouse building may be seen witchcraft documents that attract visitors from all over the world. Here, in manuscript form, are all the testimony from the witchcraft trials and the original death warrant of Bridget Bishop, who was hanged on Gallows Hill. Here too are the "witch pins" which the bewitched victims claimed were instruments of torture.

Beyond the formal Ionic porch of the modern Registry of Deeds are the records of wills and deeds dating from 1640, a happy hunting ground for antiquarians and genealogists. The resi-

The Peirce-Nichols House after a snowstorm.

dential part of Federal Street begins just west of North Street, and it is here that the stroller begins a pleasant experience. The street is filled with gracious old houses that have undergone a variety of destinies, some of them none too happy. Many of them have been carefully restored and others are waiting for new owners to bring them back to their former glory. Two Federal Street houses in particular stand out at this moment, and both of them are furnished and opened to the public under the auspices of the Essex Institute.

The Peirce-Nichols House at 80 Federal Street is the greatest treasure. Young Samuel McIntire, at the age of twenty-four, designed this superb three-story frame mansion for Jerathmeal Peirce in 1782. Peirce was a wealthy ship owner and East India merchant and his ships used to tie up in the North River just below his house. It took McIntire several years to finish the in-

Early spring at the Peirce-Nichols House.

Jerathmeal Peirce's wooden pump, stables and counting house.

terior paneling and woodwork. The house illustrates clearly the transition between the Georgian and Federal periods. The great craftsman also designed and built some of the furniture especially for this house, which has been described by many critics as the finest three-story wooden mansion in New England. In the handsome east drawing room were married George Nichols and Sally Peirce, daughter of Jerathmeal, in November 1801. At this time the owner commissioned McIntire to decorate the east rooms in his later, Federal style.

Four rooms, two on the ground floor, and two on the second, have been flawlessly restored and furnished, and these are open to the public. McIntire designed the doorways and the fence and executed the graceful urns that cap the fence posts. The Peirce-Nichols property has more than this to offer. In the rear of the house is the courtyard with Jerathmeal Peirce's counting house, his wooden pump and stables for his horses and carriages.

An earlier view of the east bedroom of the Peirce-Nichols House shows the four-post bed with a netted canopy that belonged to the Nichols family, as did the camphor-wood chest, leather covered and studded with brass nails.

In the drawing room the fine mantle is flanked by two niches containing settees made by Samuel McIntire.

A delicate McIntire doorway in the drawing room.

In the same room is an old rosewood piano made in London in the early 19th century.

The west parlor is an earlier McIntire room, distinctly Georgian in feeling.

A detail of the mantle in the west parlor showing McIntire's superb carving and design.

The cupboard contains a collection of blue Canton china of the Fitzhugh pattern.

A delicate Sheraton sofa is placed near the fireplace in the upstairs sitting room. On the wall is a banjo clock by Aaron Willard, Jr.

The Georgian mantle in the upstairs sitting room has rich, heavy moldings. The opening is framed by a set of red-orange Sadler tiles.

A recent view of the east bedroom shows a group of fine Sheraton chairs and a mahogany chest-on-chest with shell carving.

An elaborate mantle graces the east bedroom.

The central hallway offers a glimpse of a noble grandfather's clock.

Federal Street is a restful thoroughfare of sedate old houses, some well restored like these. Others patiently await badly needed restoration.

A dignified pitch-roofed frame house stands behind its picket fence at Federal and Monroe streets.

On Andover Street, which branches off from Federal Street, is the fine saltbox Abbot House, built around 1800.

The Cook-Oliver House is one of the distinguished mansions on Federal Street. It was designed by Samuel McIntire and built in 1802-3.

The Assembly House (1782).

The Assembly House at 138 Federal Street is unusual, inasmuch as it was originally planned and built, in simple form, as a Federalist club in 1782. It was intended for social assemblies, concerts, plays and dances. The Marquis de Lafayette attended a ball here in his honor in 1784 and five years later George Washington was feted in its graceful candle-lit salons. In 1795 the Assembly House was sold to Jonathan Waldo, who made it into his private dwelling. Samuel McIntire made the plans for its remodeling, which included a bright new façade with Ionic pilasters. The grape-festooned portico was added much later, after 1833. Although the building has been a private home for such a long time it still retains the atmosphere of a club, especially in the stair landing and the billiard room. After certain restorations, the Assembly House will be open to the public with early furnishings that recall Salem's maritime trade with the Far East.

Portico of the Assembly House.

The parlor of the Assembly House provides a Federalist setting for exotic pieces brought from the Orient by Salem shipmasters and merchants.

The elaborate carved table contrasts with the chaste fireplace. These pictures were taken before the recent restoration.

In the dining room of the Assembly House is a panel of colorful hand-painted Chinese paper.

At the stair landing is a most unusual formal doorway with rich Ionic pilasters and a graceful bust set in its broken pediment.

The classic Captain Benjamin Carpenter House, dating from the middle
19th century, brings this stroll along Federal Street to a close.

Essex Street at North.

A Stroll on Essex Street

Essex Street, Salem's principal thoroughfare, holds a great deal of interest for the visitor who explores the Essex Institute and the Peabody Museum but then, as he turns westward, it lapses into commercialism. Many noble old seventeenth- and eighteenth-century houses have vanished in the wake of "progress" and it is only when Essex Street crosses North Street that things take a turn for the better and the observant pedestrian can enjoy a succession of fine old buildings. Not all of them are inspiring. Some have been disfigured by nineteenth-century appendages and some of them are frankly Victorian eyesores. But the average is good, and a leisurely promenade along this broad, tree-sheltered street between North and Flint Streets will offer rich rewards. The first of them is apparent at once.

Standing on the corner is the Old Witch House at 310 Essex Street, built about 1692. This was the home of Jonathan Corwin,

The Witch House in winter.

The fireplace in the living room of the Witch House is framed in fine solid beams. The lintel is charged with a musket and powder horns in the spirit of the times.

The Lindall-Gibbs-Osgood House (1773).

one of the judges of the witchcraft court. Preliminary hearings in the witchcraft cases were said to have been held here before Judge Corwin. A Victorian drugstore protruded from this building not so long ago but it was removed and the old house was restored to its pristine state by the City of Salem. In recent years the house was capped by a gambrel roof but careful research showed that it was originally a many-gabled, almost Elizabethan house. Today it is open to the public during the warmer months, and Salem maids in appropriate costume show visitors through its ancient rooms.

Adjoining this is the dignified Lindall-Gibbs-Osgood House at 314 Essex Street, built in 1773. This was the boyhood home of Benjamin Thompson, later Count Rumford, famed as a soldier and inventor of Rumford stoves and ovens. Today it serves as headquarters for the Salem Chapter of the American Red Cross.

The First Church, at 316 Essex Street, was formed in the summer of 1629 and was the first Congregational society in America. The original meeting house was built at a different site before

First Church (Unitarian) built in 1835.

A glimpse of the Ropes Memorial and First Church.

1635; three others followed it. The present dignified granite structure, now known as First Church and a Unitarian place of worship, was built in 1835. Gridley J. F. Bryant was the architect. It has some of the atmosphere of an old English parish church, with Gothic interior finish and high-backed pews. It owns an interesting silver communion service, including two cups attributed to Paul Revere.

The Ropes Memorial at 318 Essex Street is a fine gambrel-roofed mansion guarded by richly carved fence posts. Built about 1719, it was purchased by Judge Nathaniel Ropes in 1768 and remained in the Ropes family for well over a century. During this time it was extensively rebuilt. Judge Ropes was a strong Loyalist and his house was attacked by a mob of patriots in 1774. Under a trust established by his descendants the family mansion and the surrounding garden were opened to the public in 1913. The house was moved back from its setting at the edge of the sidewalk and the handsome fence and posts were added.

The Ropes Memorial (1719).

Fronting the Ropes Memorial is one of the most memorable arrays of fence posts in New England.

A part of the display of Canton china in the Ropes Memorial.

Furnished with period pieces, the house now provides a trustworthy picture of the possessions and way of life of a prosperous Salem family in the early nineteenth century. Visitors see family portraits, old silver and costumes but the most interesting exhibit is a double set of Canton china in mint condition. This handsome china was imported in 1816 for Miss Sally Fiske Ropes when she married her cousin, Joseph Orne. She died shortly after the marriage and the china spent many undisturbed decades packed in barrels in the basement.

Both the house and the garden are open to the public, free.

The imposing Loring-Emmerton House at 328 Essex Street was the home of George Bailey Loring, a member of Congress. He also served as Commissioner of Agriculture under Presidents Garfield and Arthur, and as minister to Portugal. In this house he entertained President Pierce on several occasions and it is evident that the dignified carriage entrance served a useful purpose. In later years this was the home of Miss Caroline O. Emmerton, the philanthropist, who restored the House of Seven Gables and es-

95

The Loring-Emmerton House.

The Salem Athenaeum.

The imposing carriage entrance to the Loring-Emmerton House, with the stables beyond.

The Clark-Morgan House.

tablished the social settlement work that contributes so much felicity to that part of Salem.

The Salem Athenaeum at 339 Essex Street was incorporated in 1810. A private library, the character and contents of this organization are like the Boston Athenaeum in many respects. There are a hundred shareholders and over 30,000 volumes are available to suitably certified scholars. The present building with a classic portico dates from 1906, and the exterior bears a resemblance to "Homewood," a Baltimore mansion built in 1804.

Nathaniel Hawthorne was one of the most assiduous frequenters of the Athenaeum and withdrew an imposing number of books, the record of which may be seen in the Essex Institute. The Athenaeum prizes one of its books with Hawthorne's notes written in the margin.

Among the more attractive buildings along Essex Street is the Clark-Morgan House at No. 358. This graceful residence of

The Cabot-Endicott House (1748).

The Salem Public Library.

many pediments dates from the second quarter of the eighteenth century. The fallen leaves on the time-worn brick sidewalk give an intimation of the winter to come. The house slumps back from the vertical in the relaxed manner that is the privilege of old age. The Morgan sisters kept a Dame school here in the late nineteenth century.

The dignified and imposing Cabot-Endicott House at 365 Essex Street was built in 1748 for Joseph Cabot. Its English architect is also credited with designing "The Lindens" in Danvers, which was the country home of the Marblehead merchant prince, Robert "King" Hooper. In later years this house in Essex Street was bought by Judge William Crowninshield Endicott, Justice of the Massachusetts Supreme Court and Secretary of War under President Cleveland. Here Judge Endicott entertained General Sherman and the Right Honorable Joseph Chamberlain of England, who at a subsequent date married the Judge's daughter, Mary Crowninshield Endicott. In recent years the house served as the residence of the founder of Parker Games, one of Salem's leading industries.

Grace Church (Episcopal) and its Parish House.

Almost opposite, at 380 Essex Street, is an imposing mansion built of yellow brick.

Almost across the street, at 370 Essex Street, is the Salem Public Library. This was formerly the most imposing residence of Captain John Bertram, who was born on the Isle of Jersey and became one of Salem's greatest merchants and philanthropists. His heirs presented the house to the city in 1887. Designed by Joseph C. Foster and built in 1855, its exterior brick shell needed to be changed but slightly in adapting it to a library. But the interior floors were entirely rebuilt and large additions have been built in the rear.

Nearby, across the way at 381 Essex Street, is Grace Church, the second Episcopal edifice to stand on this site. This fine example of English Perpendicular Gothic architecture was designed by Philip Horton Smith and built in 1927. The handsome reredos was carved in Boston from English oak and the marble used for the central aisle was imported from Italy. The adjoining three-story Parish House is a much older structure, built prior to 1806. This Federal house was owned by Ebenezer Smith, who maintained a bakery in the rear.

100

The western end of Essex Street is a succession of dignified façades and graceful doorways. The fences are often elaborate and the sidewalk is usually brick.

The East India House.

There is a cluster of interesting buildings as the stroller approaches Flint Street, the most interesting being the East India House at 384 Essex Street. Parts of this red three-story dwelling, the William Stearns House, are definitely attributed to Samuel McIntire, especially the Doric doorway. One of Salem's early-eighteenth-century houses, it was built by Joseph Dean and used as a wayside inn under the name of the "East India House." It was occupied by the Spragues and their descendants, the Stearns, for ten generations. It was remodeled at the end of the eighteenth century when McIntire worked on the house. In all probability he built the front porch.

The double house at 21-23 Chestnut Street, built for Henry and John Pickering.

A Stroll on Chestnut Street

In the opinion of many qualified critics, Chestnut Street in Salem is the finest, best preserved and most aristocratic thoroughfare in America. It is not very long, but the wide, tree-shaded avenue that extends from Summer Street to Flint Street has few flaws. Only one major casualty needs to be reported—the loss by fire of the South Church. The graceful white Protestant temple designed by Samuel McIntire, which stood opposite Hamilton Hall, was destroyed by flames in 1903. The architect journeyed to Newburyport to study the Church of the First Religious Society, built in the town on Pleasant Street in 1801, and the vanished Salem church bore a strong resemblance to it, particularly the graceful spire.

Chestnut Street after a February snowstorm.

Chestnut Street is not as old as many other parts of Salem. It was laid out through fields and apple orchards near the turn of the nineteenth century, some authorities giving the date as 1796, others citing 1803. Its stately three-story mansions date from this time and from the next two or three decades. The Salem aristocrats interested in building here were the merchants and ship owners of substantial means who sought a quiet place for their homes, well removed from the wharves and counting houses. These were the people who planted the sapling elms that now arch the broad street and these were the citizens who laid out the brick sidewalks with cobblestone gutters. It is pleasant to picture the wide street in those days, its elms already towering above, when cows were driven through it to pasture, while tanner's carts, one-horse shays and an occasional stagecoach came by. Today the street is paved instead of being a simple dirt road but few other changes can be observed. There are no telephone poles, as all

Number 8 Chestnut Street, once the sexton's home.

wiring is underground. One senses the atmosphere of prosperity and calm that existed during Salem's great shipping days, when its intrepid sea captains ventured to the four corners of the earth and brought back sizeable fortunes. A story lies behind every one of these mansions with their stately doorways. These doorways, by the way, follow a variety of patterns. Many are semi-elliptical, supported by Doric and Ionic columns. Some are pedimented, with simple Doric proportions. But the more elaborate houses have rich projecting porches with railings, elliptical fanlights and sidelights as well.

Chestnut Street is a perfect place for a leisurely stroll because it is refreshingly quiet. It is not a highway and the traffic is one-way, reducing the flow of automobiles to a happy minimum. Children can play on the elm-shaded street without danger and there is room for their bicycles, hula hoops and even soft-ball games.

South Church on Chestnut Street, from
an old photograph.

Doric Doorway of Hamilton Hall.

This little guided tour begins at the eastern extremity of the thoroughfare, where Summer Street crosses it. Two conventional brick houses with arched doorways are on this corner, traditionally doctor's offices, while late-nineteenth-century dwellings are across the way. This is the older end of the avenue, and the first house of particular interest is the handsome gray edifice at Number 8. This began as a one-story brick house and was the residence of the sexton of South Church, which stood next door. The sexton was David Ashby, who slaughtered hogs and dug cellars for additional income. The date of the original house was about 1805 and the two additional stories were added in 1829.

The broad green expanse of lawn that adjoins this house is the site of South Church, the first pretentious building on Chestnut Street. Built from McIntire's inspired plans, it had a delicate and graceful steeple 163 feet high, clearly inspired by Sir Christopher Wren. Our photograph, obviously taken many years ago, shows the graceful façade with Hamilton Hall in the foreground. The church was dedicated in 1805 and was completely gutted by fire almost a century later, in 1903. A huge crowd of some 5,000 people stood in the snow and watched firemen from Salem and adjacent towns battle the blaze.

106

Hamilton Hall (1805).

Across the street from this grassy plot is Hamilton Hall, built from plans by Samuel McIntire in 1805 and named in honor of the great Federalist, Alexander Hamilton. He had often visited Salem and had many admirers there. This building has been the scene of Salem Assemblies for well over a century and a half. The Marquis de Lafayette was the guest of honor here on August 31, 1824, when 300 guests were present. Hamilton Hall is still the scene of wedding receptions, balls, lectures, anniversary dinners and even auctions, and may be considered the social heart of the North Shore.

The proposed building where men and maidens could dance was violently opposed by Dr. Hopkins, minister of South Church across Chestnut Street. In one of his sermons he declaimed: "Back to back, and breast to breast, they are dancing their souls down to hell."

107

The ballroom of Hamilton Hall, where Lafayette was entertained, and where generations of Salem belles have made their debut.

On Chestnut Street Day, a rare occasion, old costumes come out of mothballs and there is dancing in the street.

This is one of McIntire's finest designs, and the plans for it may be seen in the Essex Institute. The ballroom is illuminated in the daytime by handsome Palladian windows; two fine chandeliers brighten it at night. Salem's recent history is filled with accounts of the fashionable assemblies that were held in Hamilton Hall. Debutantes for generations have made their deep curtsies before the town dowagers standing before these ornate gilt mirrors, which were supposedly brought from Russia in 1809. The orchestra occupied a narrow balcony above the dancers. Frequent mention is made of John Remond, the colored restaurateur who catered to the assemblies and whose shop on the ground floor was famous for its turtle soup, served every morning at eleven. Throughout the years there has always been a shop or two on the ground floor of Hamilton Hall. At present it is occupied by a caterer and an antique shop of great charm.

Hamilton Hall underwent a transformation in 1844, not altogether a happy one. In recent years it had been restored to its original beauty, partly with funds raised on "Chestnut Street Day." This memorable event, which required an enormous expenditure of time and effort, has occurred at infrequent intervals. The street was closed to traffic, an admission fee was charged and most of the houses were open to the public. There was dancing in the street and Salem's best citizens were there in the costumes of their ancestors.

Three handsome and dignified mansions grace the north side of the avenue just beyond Cambridge Street. Number 10 is a fine brick house with an Ionic portico, built by Nathan Robinson in 1808. This was later the home of Philip Little, one of Salem's most celebrated marine and landscape painters. Number 12, somewhat more severe despite its Corinthian porch, was built as a two-family house by Jonathan Hodges in 1805. This is the only residence on Chestnut Street designed by Samuel McIntire. It was converted into a single-family house in 1845. Number 14 is quite different in design, with a pilastered façade and a wing that incorporates an entrance porch. This house was built on a boggy piece of land in 1835 by John C. Lee, a Boston banker, and is the best Greek Revival house on the street. Later it became the residence of Salem's great painter and etcher of wildlife, Frank W. Benson.

Winter morning on Chestnut Street with Number 18, built by James B. Bott, in the center.

Number 18, a wooden house on the corner of Botts Court, was built by James B. Bott, who maintained a saddle shop. This, probably the oldest house on Chestnut Street, was standing before the street was laid out. Nathaniel Hawthorne lived here for a short time with his family in 1847. Beyond this is a frame Greek Revival double house dating from 1836, one half of which, Number 22, is the rectory of Grace Church.

Across the street are other mansions of interest. Number 15, the one with the pleasant Doric portico, was built in 1810 by Captain Solomon Towne, a shipmaster who traveled widely and died on the coast of Sumatra. Five of his children were born in this house. Number 17, built by Captain Stephen Phillips in 1805, was long the residence of the Phillips family, one of whom was mayor of Salem. Number 19, the frame house painted chocolate and white, was built in 1805 by Charles Cleveland, a deputy collector of the port of Salem. He later became a missionary and

Number 10 Chestnut Street, has a graceful Ionic portico. In the background are Numbers 12 and 14.

Early Spring on Chestnut Street. Number 19 is in the center, dwarfed by a soaring elm.

lived to be almost a centenarian. The Roman Doric doorway is very graceful. Number 21-23 is a double brick house built in 1814-15 by Jabez Smith, a master builder, for Henry and John Pickering. When President Andrew Jackson paid a visit to Salem in 1833 he was entertained here. The two semi-elliptical Ionic doorways are dignified and well designed. Number 25, on the corner of Pickering Street, probably dates from 1802 and was built by Pickering Dodge. Its doorway is graced by rounded granite steps and delicate ironwork. Number 27, just across Pickering Street, is an immense brick house built in 1819 by Dudley Leavitt Pickman, who engaged Jabez Smith to plan and build it. The doorway is more than imposing. Next to it is Number 29, another mastodonic brick mansion. It was built for Pickering Dodge and took three years to complete, being finished in 1825. Plans were prepared by an English architect and master builder, David Lord. Many skilled woodcarvers helped on the interiors, among them Joseph McIntire, nephew of the great Samuel. Inside were installed fireplaces and mantels of white Carrara marble imported from Italy and in the cellar is a massive white marble bathtub brought from Rome. The brick walls are two feet thick. The doorway, surmounted by a Palladian window, is probably the most elaborate in Salem.

Farther along on the south side of Chestnut Street is Number 39, an early brick house painted gray and embellished with a two-and-a-half-story white porch. This was built in 1805 by Captain Thomas Saunders, whose two daughters, Mary Elizabeth and Caroline, both married Saltonstall brothers, Leverett and Nathaniel. Captain Saunders also built the large double brick house at Number 41-43 that fronts on Flint Street, and both of the young Saltonstall families lived in this house.

If you are not too footsore and weary, a few stately mansions remain to be seen on the northern side of the street. Number 26, glorying in a rich beard of ivy, is the Humphrey Devereaux House, built in 1826-27. Number 28 is the Ichabod Tucker House, built about 1800, which now serves as the parsonage for the First Church. It was remodeled and enlarged in 1846. Number 34 is the only house standing on Chestnut Street that was not originally built there. It had been a two-story house at Oak Hill in Danvers, known as the Nathaniel West House. It was cut in two

The Nathaniel West House.

and moved many miles to Salem, probably about 1824. There the two parts were erected with a wide stair hall between them and a third story was added. Once an aristocratic Salem boarding house and then a private residence, it has been empty for many years. The Ionic porch was added by its last owner, Stephen Phillips, who commissioned architect William G. Rantoul to make the design. The last house on Chestnut Street's north side is a brick structure that bears a certain resemblance to the Richard Derby House facing Derby Wharf. It was built in 1909 for the family of Miss Caroline O. Emmerton, one of Salem's great philanthropists. And there you have one of the finest streets in America, as beautiful today as it was a century ago. There is a lesson in conservation to be learned here.

A wintry glimpse of Broad Street.

Running almost parallel to Chestnut Street and south of it is Broad Street. Here the inquiring pedestrian finds several good, unpretentious eighteenth-century houses. It is a walk worth taking because it ends up in a blaze of triumph in the Pickering House, at 18 Broad Street. The pioneer of all Salem houses that are still standing, this many-gabled structure was built in 1660 by John Pickering and occupied by his lineal descendants ever since. The eleventh generation of the family now occupies the house and shows it and its noble furnishings to interested visitors by appointment. A cast-iron fireback was made for this house by Elisha Jenks, the first iron founder in the Colonies, at the Saugus Iron Works. It bears the date 1660 and may be seen in the Essex Institute.

The original old house was situated on a farm of some

The Pickering House (1660), oldest in Salem.

twenty-five acres known as "Broadlands" and many a shipmaster bought land from the Pickerings on which to build his mansion. Timothy Pickering, soldier and statesman, who occupied high cabinet posts under George Washington and John Adams, was born here in 1745. The antiquity of this steep-roofed house has been partially concealed by exterior additions made in 1841, when the current building fad was to add Gothic gingerbread trimmings to old houses. The Pickering House has survived this affront with poise and dignity.

A rare 17th-century table sits in the library of the Pickering House.

The east chamber of the Pickering House displays a noble mahogany high chest and a fireplace lined with old English tiles.

The Gedney House on High Street, near Broad, is the most recent of old Salem houses to be opened to the public. This house is very ancient, parts of it dating from 1665 when Eleazer Gedney, shipwright, began construction. His first wife, who died in 1683, was the daughter of John Turner, builder of the House of Seven Gables. A lean-to was added in the 18th century. This venerable structure has recently been rescued and restored by the Society for the Preservation of New England Antiquities. A visit to the interior will reveal many structural details in the building of a 17th-century New England house. Adjoining the Gedney House is an attractive gambrel-roofed cottage dating from 1790.

Index

(Page numbers in italics refer to illustrations)

119

120